SYMBOLS
OF
AMERICA

BY DANIEL AHEARN

BEST PRACTICES IN READING
Classroom Library

CONTENTS

A **symbol** is something that stands for something else. One symbol of America is our country's flag. Some buildings and statues are symbols of America, too. On holidays, we use these symbols to show how we feel about our country. People from all over the world know these symbols of America. Let's take a look to find out more!

THE FOURTH OF JULY

On the 4th of July, we celebrate our freedom from England. It is America's birthday. We also call it **Independence** Day. It is celebrated in many ways.

4

Families spend time together. There are parades, picnics, concerts, and fireworks. Many Americans fly flags to show how proud they feel. Everyone remembers that it is important to live in a free country.

THE AMERICAN FLAG

It is believed that in 1776, George Washington asked Betsy Ross to sew the first American flag. She was well known for her sewing. This may be why the first flag is still known as "the Betsy Ross" flag. It was red, white, and blue. It had thirteen stripes and thirteen stars. The stripes stood for the thirteen states that existed in 1776.

Today, the flag of the United States of America has fifty stars. There is one star for every state. There are still thirteen stripes to **honor** the first thirteen states. We fly the flag at our homes, schools, government buildings, sports events, and parades. The flag reminds us that we are all part of one country.

THE NATIONAL ANTHEM

In 1814, our country was again at war with England. One night, the poet Francis Scott Key saw British ships attacking an American fort. In the morning, Key saw that the American flag was still flying. He was so proud that he wrote "The Star-Spangled Banner." In 1931, Congress named "The Star-Spangled Banner" as the American national **anthem.**

These children are singing the national anthem.
Americans proudly sing the national anthem on holidays,
before sports events, and any time they want to honor our
country. When the music starts playing, Americans stand,
put their right hands over their hearts, and sing!

THE LIBERTY BELL

The **Liberty** Bell is in Philadelphia, Pennsylvania. It is very large and weighs 2,080 pounds. Millions of people still come to visit the Liberty Bell. It played a big role in American history.

Before 1776, America had been a part of England. Many Americans wanted to be free from England. On July 4th, 1776, this bell rang throughout the night. It announced the new, free nation to the American people. This is why it has been called the Liberty Bell. Even though the bell cracked long ago, it still stands as a symbol of freedom to the American people.

THE STATUE OF LIBERTY

The Statue of Liberty stands 151 feet tall in New York City's **harbor.** The statue was built in France. The French people wanted to honor America's 100th birthday. The Statue was sent to America by ship in 1876. It was so big that it had to be packed into 214 crates. The Statue was put back together in 1886.

   The Statue of Liberty is a symbol of freedom and friendship. The torch stands for the power of freedom to light the world. The torch of the statue is lit with an electric light. People can walk up stairs inside the statue. They can go inside the statue's head and look out. The Statue of Liberty still holds her torch high.

1 What are some symbols of America?

2 How does a symbol tell us something without words?

3 What do the fifty stars stand for on the American flag?

4 How do you feel when you see some of America's symbols?

PRESIDENT'S DAY

At one time there were two holidays in February celebrating the birth of past presidents. We celebrated the birthday of President Abraham Lincoln on February 12th. Then on February 22nd, we celebrated the birthday of our first president, George Washington. In 1971, President Richard Nixon decided there should be one day to honor all the past presidents of the United States. Now our nation celebrates President's Day every year on the third Monday of February.

President George Washington

Lincoln Memorial

President Abraham Lincoln

THE CAPITOL

The Capitol is one of our country's most famous buildings. It is in Washington, D.C. It was built in the 1790s. The Capitol is one of the most important symbols of American government. In 1800, **Congress** met in the Capitol for the first time. The Congress is a group of people who make our country's laws. Today, the Congress still meets in the Capitol.

Dome ceiling of Capitol

The large dome on top of the Capitol is made from almost nine million pounds of cast iron. The building has about 540 rooms, 850 doorways, and over 650 windows. The dome itself has over 100 windows! Inside, under the dome, is a large round room. This room is called the **rotunda**. In the center of the rotunda is a painting of people from America's past.

THE WHITE HOUSE

The White House is also in Washington, D.C. It has been the home of the president and his family for over 200 years. John Adams, our second president, was the first to live here.

At first, the name "White House" was a nickname, given because it was painted white. President Theodore Roosevelt made that the official name in 1901.

The White House isn't just the president's home. It is his office, too. Every year, thousands of people come to see the White House. There are 132 rooms in the White House. Some are used for the president to meet with other leaders. There are also dining rooms and guest bedrooms. Some of the rooms are named for their colors, such as the Blue Room or the Green Room.

Green Room

THE BALD EAGLE

The bald eagle was named the national bird in 1782. This eagle is found only in North America. The bald eagle stands as a symbol of American strength and peace. It was chosen as America's symbol for the Great Seal of the United States. The Great Seal also appears on our one dollar bill.

You have seen that symbols can be many things, such as a bird, a song, or even a holiday. Each symbol of America has a special meaning. Separately, they mean different things. Together, they stand for the United States of America, its history, its people, and its freedom.

GLOSSARY

anthem   song of praise or honor

Congress   group of elected men and women that make U.S. laws

harbor   protected area to anchor ships

honor   to pay great respect to

independence   freedom of a country or person

liberty   freedom from control

rotunda   large round room

symbol   something that stands for something else

INDEX